The Little Book of
ONE LINERS

D1340218

MARKS &
SPENCER

Marks and Spencer plc
PO Box 3339, Chester CH99 9QS
Copyright © Exclusive Editions 2001

shop online

www.marksandspencer.com

This book was created by Magpie Books, an imprint of Constable &
Robinson Ltd

ISBN: 978-1-84805-411-0

Printed in China

A copy of the British Library Cataloguing-in-Publication Data is
available from the British Library

Contents

Introduction

Noah was an amateur; the *Titanic* was built by professionals.

Malcolm Allison

Brilliant conversation was once an art and those with talent (Samuel Johnson, Oscar Wilde, Dorothy Parker, to name but a very few) produced some masterpieces. The Little Book of One-Liners *contains a variety of snippets ranging from the subtly clever to the vitriolic. And not only do we admire alacrity of wit but there is something about the human race that draws great amusement from the verbal slaying of others. Perhaps it is the modern equivalent of watching the Christians thrown to the lions. This collection of wicked understatement and abusive oratory should satisfy the most voracious appetite.*

Chapter 1

ARTISTIC TEMPERAMENT

Michael Caine can out-act any, well nearly any, telephone kiosk you care to mention.

Hugh Leonard

Stage and screen, music, art and literature – more inventive invective and critical commentary from those in the limelight.

They couldn't direct lemmings off a cliff.

Doug Brod

He looks like a half-melted rubber bulldog.

John Simon (of Walter Matthau)

Like a rat up a rope.

Coral Browne (of a hyperactive colleague)

The Henry Fondas lay on the evening like a damp Mackintosh.

Noël Coward

Audrey Hepburn is a walking X-ray.

Billy Wilder

Wet she was a star – dry she ain't.
> Joe Pasternak (of swimmer turned actress
> Esther Williams)

Like acting with 210 pounds of condemned veal.
> Coral Browne (of a male actor)

She was like a sinking ship, firing on the rescuers.
> Alexander Woollcott (of Mrs Patrick Campbell)

Tallulah Bankhead barged down the Nile last night
as Cleopatra – and sank.
> John Mason Brown

His features resemble a fossilized washrag.

Alan Brien (of Steve McQueen)

Barbara Cartland's eyes were twin miracles of mascara and looked like two small crows that had crashed into a chalk cliff.

Clive James

Madonna's so hairy – when she lifted her arm I thought it was Tina Turner in her armpit.

Joan Rivers

She has only two things going for her – a father and a mother.

John Simon (of Liza Minnelli)

Hollywood – they know only one word of more than one syllable here, and that is *fillum*.

Louis Sherwin

If Woody Allen didn't exist then somebody would have knitted him.

Lesley White

They shot too many pictures and not enough actors.

Walter Winchell

When I grow up, I still want to be a director.

Steven Spielberg

Editing the film *The Boy Friend*, a gorilla in boxing gloves wielding a pair of garden shears could have done a better job.

Ken Russell

Getting the costumes right in *Cleopatra* was like polishing the fish-knives on the *Titanic*.

Julian Barnes

Pardon me Ma'am, I thought you were a guy I knew in Pittsburgh.

Groucho Marx (to Greta Garbo in *Bring on the Empty Horses*)

James Cagney rolled through the film like a very belligerent barrel.

Noël Coward

The best time I ever had with Joan (Crawford) was when I pushed her down the stairs in *Whatever Happened to Baby Jane*.

Bette Davis

Ryan O'Neal is so stiff and clumsy he can't even act a part requiring him to be stiff and clumsy.

Jay Cocks

Say anything you want about me, but you make fun of my picture and you'll regret it the rest of your fat midget life.

Joshua Logan (to Truman Capote)

This is one of those films that should never have been released – not even on parole.

Christopher Tookey

Nowadays Mitchum doesn't so much act as point his suit at people.

Russell Davies

This film wasn't released – it escaped.

James Caan

Never judge a book by its movie.

J.W. Eagan

Book: what they make a movie out of for television.

Leonard Louis Levinson

To suggest that *Break A Leg* needs a splint would be to offer it an unjustifiable hope of recovery.

Clive Barnes

Cher looked like a bag of tattooed bones in a sequined slingshot.

Worst Dressed List

Marilyn Monroe was good at playing abstract confusion in the same way that a midget is good at being short.

Clive James

That's what you think!

James Agee (of the film *You Were Meant For Me*)

Television is chewing gum for the mind.

Frank Lloyd Wright

Television: an electric device which, when turned off, stimulates conversation.

Anon

He directed rehearsals with all the airy deftness of a rheumatic deacon producing *Macbeth* for a church social.

Noël Coward (of J.R. Crawford)

I think that first nights should come near the end of a play's run – as indeed they often do.

Peter Ustinov

The first rule of comedy is not to perform in a town where they still point at aeroplanes.

Bobby Mills

It was one of those plays in which all the actors unfortunately enunciated very clearly.

Robert Benchley

Since the war a terrible pall of significance has fallen over plays.

Noël Coward

You never get a chance to sit down unless you're a king.

Josephine Hull (on acting in Shakespeare's plays)

I suppose I could make changes in my play but who am I to tamper with a masterpiece.

Oscar Wilde

In this production of *Macbeth*, the prompter stole the show.

Peter Lewis

The scenery was beautiful but the actors got in front of it.

Alexander Woollcott

It's about as long as *Parsifal*, and not as funny.

Noël Coward (on *Camelot*)

Last time I performed my name was so low on the program I was getting orders for the printing.

Frank Carson

The Blaises were both a bit desiccated and lacked vitality to such a degree that one felt oxygen should be served after the fish.

Noël Coward

He played the King as though under momentary apprehension that someone else was about to play the ace.

Eugene Field (of Creston Clarke)

The press was almost unanimous on one thing, and that was that I should never have been allowed to appear in it.

Noël Coward (of his role in *London Calling*)

I look like an elderly wasp in an interesting condition.

> Mrs Patrick Campbell (of the black and yellow costume for her part in *False Gods*)

He's miscast and she's Miss Taylor.

> Emlyn Williams (of Burton and Taylor in *Private Lives*)

I've seen Don entertain fifty times and I've always enjoyed his joke.

> Johnny Carson

Lots of plays at the Royal Court are about people who talk away for hours and still can't communicate with each other.

> Noël Coward

The press is easier squashed than squared.

Winston Churchill

A critic is a man who knows the way but can't drive the car.

Kenneth Tynan

She's one great stampede from nose to navel.

Noël Coward (of an American columnist)

A censor is a man who knows more than he thinks you ought to.

Laurence J. Peter

It's the gossip columnist's business to write about what is none of his business.

Louis Kronenberger

By office boys, for office boys.

Lord Salisbury (of the *Daily Mail*)

No self-respecting fish would be wrapped in a Murdoch newspaper.

Mike Royko

You should always believe all you read in the newspapers, as this makes them more interesting.

Rose Macaulay

Every good journalist has a novel in him – which is an excellent place for it.

Russell Lynes

Journalism is unreadable, and literature is not read.

Oscar Wilde

A journalist has no ideas and the ability to express them.

Karl Kraus

Rock journalism is people who can't write interviewing people who can't talk for people who can't read.

Frank Zappa

Once a newspaper touches a story the facts are lost for ever, even to the protagonists.

Norman Mailer

Only the names have been changed, to protect the guilty.

Noël Coward
(of his short story "What Mad Pursuit")

David Halberstam's book on the 1950s, called *The Fifties*, is as inspired and clever as its title.

John Podhoretz

Your manuscript is both good and original; but the part that is good is not original, and the part that is original is not good.

Samuel Johnson

This book fills a much needed gap.

Moses Hadas

It was very intelligent and absolute rubbish.

Noël Coward (of a book written about his plays)

I have nothing to say, I am saying it and that is poetry.

John Cage

He is able to turn an unplotted, unworkable manuscript into an unplotted and unworkable manuscript with a lot of sex.

Tom Volpe (of Harold Robbins)

Although he tortures the English language, he has not yet succeeded in forcing it to reveal its meaning.

J.B. Morton

The work of a queasy undergraduate scratching his pimples.

Virginia Woolf (of James Joyce)

A louse in the locks of literature.

Alfred, Lord Tennyson (of a critic)

Very nice, though there are dull stretches.

Antoine de Rivarol (of a two-line poem)

I regard this novel as a work without any redeeming social value, unless it can be recycled as a cardboard box.

Ellen Goodman (of Danielle Steel's novel, *Message from Nam*)

Classic: a book which people praise and don't read.

Mark Twain

A writer of dictionaries, a harmless drudge.

Samuel Johnson

The way Bernard Shaw believes in himself is very refreshing in these atheistic days when so many people believe in no God at all.

Israel Zangwill

Henry James was one of the nicest old ladies I ever met.

William Faulkner

No one but a blockhead ever wrote, except for money.

Samuel Johnson

Discretion is not the better part of biography.

Lytton Strachey

In America only the successful writer is important, in France all writers are important, in England no writer is important and in Australia you have to explain what a writer is.

Geoffrey Cottrell

Should not the Society of Indexers be known as Indexers, Society of, The?

Keith Waterhouse

It's amazing how long it takes to complete something you're not working on.

R.D. Clyde

When I want to read a novel, I write one.

Benjamin Disraeli

This obscure, eccentric and disgusting poem.

Voltaire

I never read a book before reviewing it; it prejudices a man so.

Sydney Smith

Always willing to lend a helping hand to the one above him.

F. Scott Fitzgerald (of Ernest Hemingway)

For the reader who has put away comic books but isn't ready for editorials in the *Daily News*.

Gloria Steinem (of Jacqueline Susann's novel, *Valley of the Dolls*)

When Jack Benny plays the violin, it sounds as though the strings are still in the cat.

Fred Allen

Let's play a medley of your hit!

Oscar Levant (to George Gershwin)

Why do we have all these third-rate foreign conductors around when we have so many second-rate ones of our own?

Thomas Beecham

Going to the opera, like getting drunk, is a sin that carries its own punishment with it.

Hannah More

Too many pieces of music finish too long after the end.

Igor Stravinsky

Jazz will endure, as long a people hear it through their feet instead of their brains.

John Philip Sousa

If one plays good music people don't listen and if one plays bad music people don't talk.

Oscar Wilde

The English may not like music, but they absolutely love the noise it makes.

Thomas Beecham

When Brahms is in extra good spirits, he sings, *The Grave is My Joy*.

Tchaikovsky

An unalterable and unquestioned law of the musical world requires that the German text of French operas sung by Swedish artists should be translated into Italian for the clearer understanding of English speaking audiences.

Edith Wharton

He has Van Gogh's ear for music.

Orson Welles (of Donny Osmond)

The mama of Dada.

Clifton Fadiman (of Gertrude Stein)

A product of the untalented, sold by the unprincipled to the utterly bewildered.

Al Capp (of abstract art)

There are only two styles of portrait painting; the serious and the smirk.

Charles Dickens

A Realist is someone who paints what other people don't paint.

R.J. Richardson

Portrait painters tend to regard faces as not very still lives.

Alan Bennett

My art belongs to Dada.

Cole Porter (attrib.)

A tortoise-shell cat having a fit in a platter of tomatoes.

Mark Twain (on a Turner painting)

Chapter 2

~⚭~

POLITICAL OPPOSITION

There but for the grace of God goes God.
> Winston Churchill (of Stafford Cripps)

If they must stand up there on their soapboxes what else can they expect but to be knocked off? More scornful appraisals of the weaknesses and foibles of those who run the world.

Mr Speaker, I withdraw my statement that half the cabinet are asses – half the cabinet are not asses.

Benjamin Disraeli

We all know that Prime Ministers are wedded to the truth, but like other married couples they sometimes live apart.

Saki

I think it will be a clash between the political will and the administrative won't.

Jonathan Lynn and Anthony Jay, *Yes, Prime Minister*

He is going around the country stirring up apathy.

William Whitelaw (of Harold Wilson)

The Marxist law of distribution of wealth is that shortages will be divided equally among the peasants.

John Guftason

He played too much football without a helmet.

Lyndon B. Johnson (of Gerald Ford)

Had he been a much worse man he would have done Canada much less harm.

Sir Richard Cartwright (of John A. Macdonald)

He is a self-made man and worships his creator.

Benjamin Disraeli (of John Bright)

If voting changed anything they'd make it illegal.

Anon

He is forever poised between a cliché and an indiscretion.

> Harold Macmillan

He is a sheep in sheep's clothing.

> Winston Churchill (of Clement Attlee)

A Byzantine logothete.

> Theodore Roosevelt (of Woodrow Wilson)

A sophistical rhetorician, inebriated with the exuberance of his own verbosity.

> Benjamin Disraeli (of William Gladstone)

It's a recession when your neighbor loses his job; it's a depression when you lose yours.

Harry S. Truman

His mind is a muskeg of mediocrity.

John Macnaughton

In war you don't have to be nice; you only have to be right.

Winston Churchill

He can compress the most words into the smallest ideas better than any man I ever met.

Abraham Lincoln

When the eagles are silent the parrots begin to jabber.
Winston Churchill

The juvenile lead.
Aneurin Bevan (of Anthony Eden)

A Conservative is a man who's too cowardly to fight and too fat to run.
Elbert Hubbard

Sir Stafford has a brilliant mind – until it is made up.
Violet Bonham Carter (of Stafford Cripps)

They are not fit to manage a whelk-stall.
Winston Churchill (of the British Labour Party)

Ronald Reagan is a triumph of the embalmer's art.

Gore Vidal

Fleas can be taught nearly anything that a Congressman can.

Mark Twain

If the Republicans will stop telling lies about the Democrats, we will stop telling the truth about them.

Adlai Stevenson

There is only one thing worse than fighting with allies, and that is fighting without them.

Winston Churchill

It is not enough to have every intelligent person in the country voting for me – I need a majority.

Adlai Stevenson

He always played the game and he always lost it.

Winston Churchill (of Austen Chamberlain)

Ronald Reagan doesn't dye his hair, he's just prematurely orange.

Gerald Ford (attrib.)

Now that I am no longer President, I find that I do not win every game of golf I play.

George Bush

I don't think Kenneth Baker has a haircut, I think he just has an oil change.

Anon

Greater love hath no man than this, that he laid down his friends for his life.

Jeremy Thorpe (of Harold Macmillan)

If Gladstone fell into the Thames, that would be a misfortune, and if anybody pulled him out, that, I suppose, would be a calamity.

Benjamin Disraeli

Clement Attlee is a modest little man with much to be modest about.

Winston Churchill

A politician will double cross that bridge when he comes to it.

Oscar Levant

A politician will always be there when he needs you.

Ian Walsh

I cannot bring myself to vote for a woman who has been voice-trained to speak to me as though my dog had just died.

Keith Waterhouse (of Margaret Thatcher)

Clement Attlee reminds me of a dead fish before it has had time to stiffen.

George Orwell

He is a man suffering from petrified adolescence.

Aneurin Bevan (of Winston Churchill)

Choosing between Bush, Clinton and Perot was like needing clean underwear but being forced to decide between three dirty pairs.

Michael Dalton Johnson

Politics is the conduct of public affairs for private advantage.

Ambrose Bierce

Politics is derived from two words – poly, meaning many, and tics, meaning small blood-sucking insects.

Chris Clayton

Democracy: the worship of jackals by jackasses.

H.L. Mencken

Washington couldn't tell a lie, Nixon couldn't tell the truth and Reagan couldn't tell the difference.

Mort Sahl

The Secret Service is under orders if Bush is shot, to shoot Quayle.

John Kerrey

A choice between the lesser of two weevils.

S.J. Perelman (of Gerald Ford and Jimmy Carter)

Military intelligence is a contradiction in terms.

Oswald G. Villard

In Pierre Elliott Trudeau, Canada has at last produced a political leader worthy of assassination.

Irving Layton

Al Gore is in danger of becoming all things to no people.

Paul Bograd

He proves that no shirt is too young to be stuffed.

Larry Zolf (of Joe Clark)

Bill Clinton's foreign policy stems mainly from having breakfast at the International House of Pancakes.

Pat Buchanan

I am opposed by all the short-haired women and the long-haired men in the Province.

Sir Rodmond Roblin

Ronald Reagan is remarkably fit, but he doesn't cup his hand to his ear as a sunshade.

Sam Donaldson

Dan Quayle taught the kids a valuable lesson: if you don't study you could wind up as Vice-President.

Jay Leno

Chapter 3

BATTLE OF THE SEXES

Scratch a lover, and find a foe.

Dorothy Parker

Men v women, women v men, marriage, divorce and a healthy batch of put-downs.

His wife said she wanted an animal fur, so he bought her a donkey jacket.

Anon

I don't like all-in wrestling – if it's all in, why wrestle?

Mae West

If you're afraid of loneliness, don't marry.

Anton Chekhov

Familiarity breeds contempt – and children.

Mark Twain

Ask him the time and he'll tell you how the watch was made.

Jane Wyman (of ex-husband Ronald Reagan)

Fred Astaire was great, but don't forget that Ginger Rogers did everything that he did, backwards and in high heels.

Bob Thaves

You stay here for a moment while I go up and fetch my etchings.

James Thurber

In Hollywood, marriage is a success if it outlives milk.

Rita Rudner

If only he'd wash his neck, I'd wring it.

Anon

Brigands demand your money or your life; women require both.

Samuel Butler

Women want mediocre men, and men are working hard to be as mediocre as possible.

Margaret Mead

If I throw a stick will you leave?

Anon

Twenty million women rose to their feet with the cry "We will not be dictated to", and promptly became stenographers.

> G.K. Chesterton (on Women's Lib)

Men are like car alarms – they both make a lot of noise no one listens to.

> Diana Jordan

Another instance of the triumph of hope over experience.

> Samuel Johnson (of the remarriage
> of a widowed friend)

Madam, don't you have any unexpressed thoughts?

> George S. Kaufman

Women are more irritable than men, probably because men are more irritating.

Anon

You remind me of my brother – only he has a human head.

Judy Tenuta

When a man steals your wife, there is no better revenge than to let him keep her.

Sacha Guitry

Don't imagine you can change a man, unless he's in nappies.

Jasmine Birtles

The only way to get rid of cockroaches is to tell them you want a long term relationship.

Jasmine Birtles

All men are of the same mould but some are mouldier than others.

Anon

I suppose true sexual equality will come when a general called Anthea is found having an unwise lunch with a young, unreliable male model from Spain.

John Mortimer

A divorce costs much more than a wedding but it's worth it.

Anon

Why should women mind if men have their faces on the money as long as we have our hands on it?

Ivy Priest

The weaker sex are the stronger sex because of the weakness of the stronger sex for the weaker sex.

Anon

If you think women are the weaker sex, try pulling the blankets back to your side.

Stuart Turner

I'm trying to imagine you with a personality.

Anon

We pondered whether to take a holiday or get a divorce, and we decided that a trip to Bermuda is over in two weeks, but a divorce is something you always have.

Woody Allen

The hardest task in a girl's life is to prove to a man that his intentions are serious.

Helen Rowland

Is it time for your medication or mine?

Anon

One of the most difficult things in this world is to convince a woman that even a bargain costs money.

Edgar Howe

Marriage is not all bed and breakfast.

R. Coulson

Instead of getting married again, I'm going to find a woman I don't like and give her a house.

Lewis Grizzard

Divorce is the best way of getting rid of a tiresome mother-in-law.

Anon

And the judge said "All the money and we'll shorten it to alimony."

Robin Williams

Macho does not prove mucho.

Zsa Zsa Gabor

The critical period in matrimony is breakfast time.

A.P. Herbert

At whatever stage you apologize to your wife, the answer is always the same: "It's too late now."

Denys Parsons

I married beneath me, all women do.

Nancy Astor

The feminine vanity case is the grave of masculine illusions.

Helen Rowland

English is called the mother tongue because father seldom gets a chance to use it.

Anon

Always suspect any job men willingly vacate for women.

Jill Tweedie

Marriage is an attempt to turn a night owl into a homing pigeon.

Anon

Il n'y a point de héros pour son valet de chambre.
No man is a hero to his valet.

Madame Cornuel

It isn't premarital sex if you have no intention of getting married.

Matt Barry

A good husband is one who will wash up when asked and dry up when told.

Anon

The great secret of a successful marriage is to treat all disasters as incidents and none of the incidents as disasters.

Harold Nicolson

The most difficult year of marriage is the one you're in.

Anon

After a man is married he has the legal right to deceive only one woman.

Edgar Howe

Holy Deadlock.

A.P. Herbert

No nice men are good at getting taxis.

Katharine Whitehorn

Never trust a husband too far, nor a bachelor too near.

Helen Rowland

Madam, before you flatter a man so grossly to his face, you should consider whether or not your flattery is worth having.

Samuel Johnson

The female sex has no greater fan than I, and I have the bills to prove it.

Alan Jay Lerner

Give a man a free hand and he'll run it all over you.

Mae West

A husband is what is left of a lover, after the nerve has been extracted.

Helen Rowland

A woman told me she would fulfil my ultimate fantasy for £100 – so I asked her to paint my house.

Sean O'Bryan

Chapter 4

THAT'S LIFE

If you think nobody cares whether you are alive or dead, try missing a couple of car payments.

Ann Landers

Some scathing statements and philosophical fillips on the comedy of human living: money, religion, sport, people and places (not without a smattering of xenophobia), food and drink, age, health and death.

It was one of those perfect summer days – the sun was shining, a breeze was blowing, the birds were singing and the lawnmower was broken.

James Dent

How is it that the first piece of luggage on the airport carousel never belongs to anyone?

George Roberts

Life is something to do when you can't get to sleep.

Fran Lebowitz

The consumer isn't a moron; she is your wife.

David Ogilvy

If you don't drink, smoke or drive a car, you're a tax evader.

Tom Foley

Hardware is the part of the computer than can be kicked.

Jeff Pesis

History is nothing but the soul's old wardrobe.

Heinrich Heine

Never let the facts get in the way of a good story.

Anon

Sending men to that army is like shoveling fleas across a barnyard – not half of them get there.

Abraham Lincoln (of General McClellan's army)

You may know by my size that I have a kind of alacrity in sinking.

William Shakespeare

Every man has the right to be conceited until he is successful.

Benjamin Disraeli

I'm not tense, just terribly, terribly alert.

Anon

Perennials are the ones that grow like weeds, biennials are the ones that die this year instead of next and hardy annuals are the ones that never come up at all.

Katharine Whitehorn

I am determined to travel through life first class.

Noël Coward

When Soloman said there was a time and a place for everything, he had not encountered the problem of parking an automobile.

Bob Edwards

A man described as a 'sportsman' is generally a bookmaker who takes actresses to night clubs.

Jimmy Cannon

Please don't ask me to relax – it's only the tension that's holding me together.

Helen Murray

Patience: a minor form of despair, disguised as a virtue.

Ambrose Bierce

A neurosis is a secret you don't know you're keeping.

Kenneth Tynan

I'm trusting in the Lord and a good lawyer.

Oliver North

I have a previous engagement which I will make as soon as possible.

John Barrymore (to an unwanted invitation)

Conscience is the inner voice which warns us that somebody may be looking.

H.L. Mencken

Genius is one per cent inspiration, ninety-nine per cent perspiration.

Thomas Alva Edison

If it squirms, it's biology; if it stinks, it's chemistry; if it doesn't work, it's physics and if you can't understand it, it's mathematics.

Magnus Pyke

One of the worst aspects of modern English life is that so many of one's friends have to work and they're so bad at it.

Noël Coward

Science is his forte, and omniscience his foible.

Sydney Smith (of William Whewell)

A gossip is one who talks to you about other people; a bore is one who talks about himself; a brilliant conversationalist is one who talks to you about yourself.

William King

He listens to his psychiatrist, and then draws his own confusions.

Anon

Keep a diary and some day it'll keep you.

Mae West

Good people sleep better than bad people, but bad people enjoy the waking hours much more.

Woody Allen

I refuse to endure months of expensive humiliation only to be told that at the age of four I was in love with my rocking-horse.

Noël Coward

Early to bed and early to rise probably indicates unskilled labour.

John Ciardi

Assassination is the extreme form of censorship.

George Bernard Shaw

Imprisoned in every fat man a thin one is wildly signalling to be let out.

Cyril Connolly

Several excuses are always less convincing than one.

Aldous Huxley

Seriousness is stupidity sent to college.

P.J. O'Rourke

History repeats itself; historians repeat each other.

Philip Guedalla

Haste is the mother of imperfection.

Anon

Excuse me, my leg has gone to sleep – do you mind if I join it?

Alexander Woollcott (to a person
boring him at a party)

As guests go, you wish he would.

Anon

Aye, they say the new striker I'm opposing is fast – but how fast can he limp?

Mick McCarthy

He has impeccable bad taste.

Otis Ferguson

I never forget a face, but in your case I'll be glad to make an exception.

Groucho Marx

You blocks, you stones, you worse than senseless things!

William Shakespeare

He climbed the ladder of success kissing the feet of the one ahead of him and kicking the head of the one behind.

Anon

Why do you sit there looking like an envelope without any address on it?

Mark Twain

He never goes back on his word – without consulting his lawyer.

Anon

They claim to be he-men, but the hair from their combined chests wouldn't have made a wig for a grape.

Robert Benchley

He gets offended when others talk whilst he's interrupting.

Anon

Nothing is more responsible for the good old days than a bad memory.

Frank P. Adams

I do desire we may be better strangers.

William Shakespeare

She walked across the ballroom as if she were trudging through deep snow.

Noël Coward

He's a real big gun – of small calibre and immense bore.

Anon

If you're enjoying yourself in his company, it's all you're enjoying.

Anon

Unspeakable, like a hedgehog all in primroses.
Nancy Mitford (of Princess Margaret)

When there's nothing more to be said, he'll still be saying it.

Anon

He was dull in a new way, and that made many people think him great.
Samuel Johnson (of Thomas Gray)

His egotism is a plain case of mistaken nonentity.

Anon

Sweep on, you fat and greasy citizens.

William Shakespeare (from *Antony and Cleopatra*)

He had a degree so he could ice cakes with joined-up writing.

A.A. Gill

I don't know why she has such objections to birth control; she's a living argument for it.

Anon

That indefatigable and unsavoury engine of pollution, the dog.

John Sparrow

It's surprising how such a big head holds such a small brain.

Anon

You're a parasite for sore eyes.

Gregory Ratoff

The aristocracy is composed chiefly of asses – asses who talk about horses.

Heinrich Heine

Jogging is for people who aren't intelligent enough to watch television.

Victoria Wood

My face looks like a wedding cake left out in the rain.

W.H. Auden

He lights up a room when he leaves it.

Anon

Have some tongue, like cures like.

Robert Yelverton Tyrrell
(to a boring dining companion)

He has attained such a depth of seediness that a flock of starlings could feed off him.

Clive James

When a bore leaves the room, you feel as if someone came in.

Anon

Only dull people are brilliant at breakfast.

Oscar Wilde

I used to think the only use for sport was to give small boys something else to kick besides me.

Katharine Whitehorn

Golf is a good walk spoiled.

Mark Twain

Eamon D'Arcy has a golf swing like an octopus falling out of a tree.

David Feherty

The trouble with jogging is that by the time you realize you're not fit enough to do it, it's a long walk home.

Anon

The uglier a man's legs are, the better he plays golf – it's almost a law.

H.G. Wells

Ballesteros hits the ball further than I go on my holidays.

Lee Trevino

If you think it's difficult to meet new people, try picking up the wrong golf ball.

Jack Lemmon

Like a Volvo, Borg is rugged, has good after-sales service and is very dull.

Clive James

Joggers are basically neurotic, bony, smug types who could bore the paint off a DC-10.

Rick Reilly

He loved to walk sideways towards them, like a grimly playful crab.

R.C. Robertson-Glasgow
(of George Gunn's bowling technique)

I do not participate in any sport that has ambulances at the bottom of the hill.

Erma Bombeck

I don't drop players – I make changes.

Bill Shankly

I don't think the discus will ever attract any interest until we start throwing them at each other.

Al Oerter

Reality: a delusion created by an alcohol deficiency.

Anon

I saw a notice which said "Drink Canada Dry" so I've started.

Brendan Behan

All I can say is that I have taken more out of alcohol than alcohol has taken out of me.

Winston Churchill

It's always hard to see hope with a hangover.

P.J. O'Rourke

His favourite drink is the next one.

Anon

There is no such thing as a small whiskey.

Oliver St John Gogarty

You're not drunk if you can lie on the floor without holding on.

> Dean Martin

He goes into a bar optimistically and comes out misty optically.

> Anon

We drink one another's healths, and spoil our own.

> Jerome K. Jerome

I always wake up at the crack of ice.

> Joe E. Lewis

I'm only a beer teetotaller, not a champagne teetotaller.

George Bernard Shaw

Let's get out of these wet clothes and into a dry Martini.

Mae West

A woman drove me to drink and I never even had the courtesy to thank her.

W.C. Fields

But I'm not so think as you drunk I am.

J.C. Squire

Work is the curse of the drinking classes.

Oscar Wilde

A good rule is to state that the bouquet is better than the taste, and vice versa.

Stephen Potter

Food is an important part of a balanced diet.

Fran Lebowitz

I go by tummy-time and I want my dinner.

Winston Churchill

Never serve oysters in a month that has no paycheck in it.

P.J. O'Rourke

The cook was a good cook as cooks go; and as good cooks go, she went.

Saki

When I ask for a watercress sandwich I do not mean a loaf with a field in the middle of it.

Oscar Wilde

I went to a restaurant that serves "breakfast at any time" – so I ordered French Toast during the Renaissance.

Steven Wright

The murals in restaurants are about on a par with the food in art galleries.

Peter De Vries

The Hotel Carvery – as much gristle and cornflour as you can stuff down for a tenner.

A.A. Gill

I think a grave has walked over this goose.

Noël Coward

This was a good dinner enough, to be sure; but it was not a dinner to ask a man to.

Samuel Johnson

I never drink water – look at the way it rusts pipes.

W.C. Fields

Whom the gods wish to destroy they first call promising.

Cyril Connolly

An expert is one who knows more and more about less and less.

Anon

No one with a specialty can hope to have a monopoly of it.

Mark Twain

However harmless a thing is, if the law forbids it most people will think it wrong.

W. Somerset Maugham

An uneasy conscience is a hair in the mouth.

Mark Twain

Success is the one unpardonable sin against our fellows.

Ambrose Bierce

We used to build civilizations; now we build shopping malls.

Bill Bryson

There's a big difference between free speech and cheap talk.

Anon

It takes more hot water to make cold water hot than it takes to make hot water cold.

Larry Dowd

Circumstances make man, not man circumstances.

Mark Twain

A boss is a person who's early when you're late and late when you're early.

Anon

Be not afraid of going slowly, only of standing still.

Chinese proverb

Culture: a thin veneer easily soluble in alcohol.

Anon

Existentialism means that no one else can take a bath for you.

Delmore Schwartz

Envy is an admission of inferiority.

Victor Hugo

Everyone sits in the prison of his own ideas.

Albert Einstein

Not in doing what you like best, in liking what you do is the secret of happiness.

J.M. Barrie

Scandal: something that has to be bad to be good.

Anon

Anger makes dull men witty, but it keeps them poor.

Francis Bacon

It is impossible to enjoy idling thoroughly unless one has plenty of work to do.

Jerome K. Jerome

Calamities are of two kinds: misfortune to ourselves, and good fortune to others.

Ambrose Bierce

Humour is emotional chaos remembered in tranquillity.

James Thurber

One of the most difficult things to give away is kindness – it is usually returned.

Anon

If you want the last word in an argument say: "I expect you're right."

Anon

You know what they say, if at first you don't succeed, you're not the only son.

Stephen Fry

If at first you don't succeed – you're fired.

Jen Graman

A camel is a horse designed by a committee.

Alec Issigonis

It was beautiful and simple as all truly great swindles are.

O. Henry

A home keeps you from living with your parents.

P.J. O'Rourke

As one door closes, another slams in your face.

Rachel Heyhoe Flint

A door is what a dog is perpetually on the wrong side of.

Ogden Nash

Nothing is impossible for people who don't have to do it themselves.

Anon

On the day of victory, no fatigue is felt.

Arabic proverb

After you've heard two eyewitness accounts of an accident, it makes you wonder about history.

Dave Barry

A committee is an animal with four back legs.

John Le Carré

Mankind is divisible into two classes: hosts and guests.

Max Beerbohm

We ought never do wrong when people are looking.

Mark Twain

Absurdity: a statement of belief inconsistent with one's own opinion.

Anon

There is sufficiency in the world for man's need but not for man's greed.

Mahatma Gandhi

Better to keep your mouth shut and appear stupid than to open it and remove all doubt.

Mark Twain

If you don't believe in the resurrection of the dead, look at any office at quitting time.

Robert Townsend

The impossible: something that nobody can do – until somebody does it.

Anon

Don't let yesterday take up too much of today.

Will Rogers

Foolproof systems do not take into account the ingenuity of fools.

Gene Brown

Make three correct guesses consecutively and everyone will regard you as an expert.

Anon

There's only one thing in the world worse than being talked about and that is not being talked about.

Oscar Wilde

You will always find a few Eskimos ready to tell the Congolese how to cope with the heat.

Stanislaw Lec

It's a funny old world – a man's lucky if he gets out of it alive.

Walter de Leon and Paul M. Jones

Blessed is he who, having nothing to say, abstains from giving evidence of that fact.

George Eliot

A wit with dunces, and a dunce with wits.

Alexander Pope

The trouble with the rat-race is that even if you win, you're still a rat.

Lily Tomlin

All you need to grow fine, vigorous grass is a crack in your sidewalk.

James Hewett

There are only two types of exercise in Hollywood: jogging and helping a divorced friend move.

Robert Wagner

What a pity it is that we have no amusements in England but vice and religion.

Sydney Smith

London! Dirty little pool of life.

B.M. Malabari

Poms don't have much imagination because they've pinched most of their street names off the Monopoly board.

Paul Hogan

England and America are two countries divided by a common language.

George Bernard Shaw

An Englishman, even if he is alone, forms an orderly queue of one.

George Mikes

The Irish are a fair people; they never speak well of one another.

Samuel Johnson

The best thing I know between France and England is – the sea.

Douglas Jerrold

California is a fine place to live – if you happen to be an orange.

Fred Allen

The French don't care what they do as long as they pronounce it properly.

George Bernard Shaw

If ever there was an aviary overstocked with jays it is that Yaptown-on-the-Hudson called New York.

O. Henry

Canadians are Americans with no Disneyland.

Margaret Mahy

At its worst, the broad Australian accent is reminiscent of a dehydrated crow uttering its last statement on life from the bough of a dead tree in the middle of a clay-pan at the peak of a seven-year drought.

Buzz Kennedy

Waiting for the German verb is surely the ultimate thrill.

Flann O'Brien

I once heard a Californian student in Heidelberg say, in one of his calmest moods, that he would rather decline two drinks than one German adjective.

Mark Twain

Norway – the sun never sets, the bar never opens, and the whole country smells of kippers.

Evelyn Waugh

There are in England sixty different religious sects and only one sauce.

Caracciolo

I look upon Switzerland as an inferior sort of Scotland.

Sydney Smith

In India, "cold weather" is merely a conventional phrase and has come into use through the necessity of having some way to distinguish between weather which will melt a brass door knob and weather which only makes it mushy.

Mark Twain

American women expect to find in their husbands the perfection that English women only hope to find in their butlers.

W. Somerset Maugham

Americans love ice and hate cold water and so the swimming pools are as hot as bouillabaisse.

Noël Coward

Belgium is a country invented by the British to annoy the French.

Charles de Gaulle

I know why the sun never sets on the British Empire: God wouldn't trust an Englishman in the dark.

Duncan Spaeth

There is nothing the British like more than a bloke who comes from nowhere, makes it and then gets clobbered.

Melvyn Bragg

You cannot underestimate the intelligence of the American people.

H.L. Mencken

There are only two classes of person in New South Wales – those who have been convicted and those who ought to have been.

Lachlan MacQuarie

The French are the masters of "the dog ate my homework" school of diplomatic relations.

P.J. O'Rourke

The perfidious, haughty, savage, disdainful, stupid, slothful, inhospitable, inhuman English.

Julius Caesar Scaliger

An Englishman's real ambition is to get a railway compartment to himself.

Ian Hay

If someone says: "It's not the money, it's the principle," it's the money.

Angelo Valenti

It's not that it is so good with money, but that it's so bad without it.

Anon

Money makes money and the money money makes makes money.

Benjamin Franklin

If economists were any good at business, they would be rich men instead of advisers to rich men.

Kirk Kerkorian

Adults are just kids who owe money.

Anon

A bank is a place that will lend you money if you can prove that you don't need it.

Bob Hope

I wish the banks would just say, "Look you ****, line up there, we don't give a **** about your miserable little bank account."

Paul Fussell

Prosperity is the best protector of principle.

Mark Twain

When a man tells you he got rich by hard work, just ask him whose.

Anon

The two most beautiful words in the English language are "Check Enclosed."

Dorothy Parker

Death is the most convenient time to tax rich people.

David Lloyd George

I started out with nothing and I've still got most of it left.

Anon

Where there's a will there are relations.

Michael Gill

Business conventions are important because they demonstrate how many people a company can operate without.

J.K. Galbraith

Expenditure rises to meet income.

C. Northcote Parkinson

Some people go to church only when they are being baptized, married or buried – hatched, matched and dispatched.

James Hewett

It only rains straight down – God doesn't do windows.

Steven Wright

I am always most religious upon a sunshiny day.

Lord Byron

He prays on his knees on Sunday and on everybody the rest of the week.

Anon

It is no accident that the symbol of a bishop is a crook and the symbol of an archbishop is a double-cross.

Gregory Dix

The easy confidence with which I know another man's religion is folly teaches me to suspect that my own is also.

Mark Twain

God is a man, so it must be all rot.

Nancy Nicholson

God will pardon me, it is His trade.

Heinrich Heine

Thanks to God, I am still an atheist.

Luis Buñuel

If God had meant us to walk around naked, he would never have invented the wicker chair.

Erma Bombeck

God is not dead but alive and working on a much less ambitious project.

Anon

Baptists are only funny underwater.

Neil Simon

Protestant women may take the pill whilst Catholic women must keep taking The Tablet.

Irene Thomas

A Christian is a man who feels repentance on a Sunday for what he did on Saturday and is going to do on Monday.

Thomas Ybarra

Maturity is a high price to pay for growing up.

Tom Stoppard

Old age isn't so bad when you consider the alternative.

Maurice Chevalier

By the time a person gets to greener pastures, he can't climb the fence.

Anon

Don't worry about senility – when it hits you, you won't know it.

Bill Cosby

Either he's dead, or my watch has stopped.

Groucho Marx

Two things grow weaker with the years – teeth and memory.

Anon

Excuse my dust.

Dorothy Parker (suggested epitaph)

To me old age is always fifteen years older than I am.

Bernard Baruch

Wrinkles merely indicate where smiles have been.

Mark Twain

I'm at the age where my back goes out more than I do.

Phyllis Diller

I got fired because of my age – I'll never make the mistake of being seventy again.

Casey Stengel

The report of my death was an exaggeration.

Mark Twain

Death is nature's way of telling you to slow down.

Anon

Memorial services are the cocktail party of the geriatric set.

Ralph Richardson

Here am I, dying of a hundred good symptoms.

Alexander Pope

Immortality is the condition of a dead man who does not believe he is dead.

H.L. Mencken

I have overcome my will-power and have taken up smoking again.

Mark Twain

As a teenager you are in the last stage of life when you will be happy to hear that the phone is for you.

Fran Lebowitz

Drugs have taught an entire generation of English kids the metric system.

P.J. O'Rourke

If I wanted to hear the pitter patter of tiny feet I'd put shoes on my cat.

Anon

Even when freshly washed and relieved of all obvious confections, children tend to be sticky.

Fran Lebowitz

The only advantage to being an adult is that you can eat your dessert without having eaten your vegetables.

Lisa Alther

Children are given us to discourage our better emotions.

Anon

Money isn't everything, but it sure keeps you in touch with your children.

J. Paul Getty

To be a successful father, there's one absolute rule: when you have a kid, don't look at it for the first two years.

Ernest Hemingway

It is not advisable to put your head around your child's door to see if it is asleep – it was.

Faith Hines

My mother loved children – she would have given anything if I had been one.

Groucho Marx

Telling a teenager the facts of life is like giving a fish a bath.

Arnold Glasow

Parents are the very last people who should be allowed to have children.

Anon

Ask your child what he wants for dinner only if he's buying.

Fran Lebowitz

Some parents have difficulty deciding on a name for the new baby, but others have rich relatives.

Don McElroy

Always obey your parents, when they are present.

Mark Twain

I don't believe in smacking children – I just use a cattle prod.

Jenny Eclair

Perhaps host and guest is really the happiest relation for father and son.

Evelyn Waugh

Children despise their parents until the age of forty, when they suddenly become just like them, thus preserving the system.

Quentin Crewe

If that's mink she's wearing, some rabbit must be living under an assumed name.

Anon

Women give themselves to God when the devil wants nothing more from them.

Sophie Arnould

The "g" is silent – the only part of her that is.

Julie Burchill (of Camille Paglia)

She has a face like a well-kept grave.

Anon

Show me a woman who doesn't feel guilt and I'll show you a man.

Erica Jong

When women go wrong, men go right after them.

Mae West

Her once dangerous curves have become extended detours.

Anon

She wears too much of not enough.

Anon

She has no heart but her brains are in the right place.

Cyril Asquith (of Diana Manners)

A woman without a man is like a fish without a bicycle.

Gloria Steinem (attrib.)

She wears the kind of dresses that start late and end early.

Anon

A man without a woman is like a moose without a hat-rack.

Arthur Marshall

She knows how to hang on to her youth – she never introduces him to other women.

Anon

Outside every thin girl there's a fat man trying to get in.

Katharine Whitehorn

The only thing that can cheat her out of the last word is an echo.

Anon

She finally admitted she was forty, but she didn't say when.

Anon

I refuse to admit that I'm more than fifty-two, even if that does make my sons illegitimate.

Nancy Astor

She dresses for the nuclear age – with fifty per cent fall out.

Anon

I wanted to marry her ever since I saw the moonlight shining on the barrel of her father's shotgun.

Eddie Albert

She's not what she was fifteen years ago – she's nine years older.

Anon

Some extraordinarily unlikely women do have it.

Noël Coward (on sex appeal)

She wears the kind of bikini that's based on the theory that nothing succeeds like nothing.

Anon

The best way for her to save face is to keep the lower half shut.

Anon

Englishwomen's shoes look like they were made by someone who had heard shoes described but had never seen any.

Margaret Halsey

Nobody loves a fairy when she's forty.

Arthur W.D. Henley

She's aged more than her husband, but less often.

Anon

Don't get too friendly with her dear, or she'll make a nest in your hair.

Noël Coward

Well, this day was a total waste of make-up.

Anon

The best years of her life were the ten between twenty-nine and thirty.

Anon

Her hat looks as if it had made a forced landing on her head.

Anon

Old blondes never fade – they just dye away.

Anon

Chapter 5

JUST RIDICULOUS

There are just two rules for success: 1. Never tell all you know.

Robert H. Lincoln

A collection of bizarre sayings – the things we find funny without really knowing why, as well as some "foot in mouth" comments which their owners will have wished they hadn't said.

I'm going to memorize your name then throw my head away.

Oscar Levant

Where I come from, the valleys are so narrow that the dogs wag their tails up and down.

Sam Snead

The moon may be smaller than the earth, but it's further away.

Steven Wright

If you get to be one hundred you've got it made – very few people die past that age.

George Burns

I could see that, if not actually disgruntled, he was far from gruntled.

P.G. Wodehouse

Most people who are as attractive, witty and intelligent as I am are usually conceited.

Joan Rivers

The Venus de Milo is a good example of what happens to somebody who won't stop biting her fingernails.

Will Rogers

I used to think that the human brain was the most fascinating part of the body and then I realized, "What is telling me that?"

Emo Phillips

"I digress," as the bride said when she got up in the middle of the night and baked a cake.

Noël Coward

Passionate hatred can give meaning and purpose to an empty life.

Eric Hoffer

There is no housing shortage in England today – it's just a rumour put about by people who have nowhere to live.

G.L. Murfin

If I am ever stuck on a respirator or a life support system, I definitely want to be unplugged, but not until I get down to a size eight.

Henriette Mantel

Alas poor Yorlik, I knew him backwards.

Anon

I'm not bald – my head is just a solar panel for a sex machine.

Telly Savalas

A bore: someone who talks when you want him to listen.

Ambrose Bierce

If the garbage man calls, tell him we don't want any.

Groucho Marx

I don't go to my psychiatrist any more – he was meddling too much in my private life.

Anon

Old MacDonald was dyslexic, IEIEO.

Billy Connolly

What's another word for Thesaurus?

Anon

Cocaine is God's way of saying you're making too much money.

Robin Williams

Reality is for people who can't face drugs.

Laurence Peter

I'd stay away from Ecstasy – it's a drug so strong it makes white people think they can dance.

Lenny Henry

Anybody who isn't pulling his weight is probably pushing his luck.

Anon

One of us must go.

Oscar Wilde (of the wallpaper which he could see from his deathbed)

He sneaked his girl out of the nudist camp because he wanted to see what she looked like in a bathing suit.

Anon

Pedestrian: someone who thought he had petrol in his tank.

Anon

Policemen, like red squirrels, must be protected.

Joe Orton

Dolphins are so intelligent that within only a few weeks they can train a man to throw fish at them from the side of a pool.

Anon

Eyewitnesses were on the scene in minutes.

Adam Boulton

If Gloria hadn't divorced me she might never have become her own daughter-in-law.

Cy Howard (of his ex-wife who married Howard's son)

First things first, second things never.

Shirley Conran

The only thing in my life that I regret is that I once saved David Frost from drowning.

Peter Cook

I learned law so well, the day I graduated I sued the college and got my tuition fees back.

Fred Allen

I would have killed myself but my analyst was a strict Freudian and if you kill yourself they make you pay for the sessions you miss.

Woody Allen

Ignorance of the law must not prevent the losing lawyer from collecting his fee.

John Mortimer

Recreations: growling, prowling, scowling and owling.

Nicholas Fairbairn's entry in *Who's Who*

This is the sort of English up with which I will not put.

Winston Churchill

Coincide: what you do when it starts raining.

Anon

The insurance man told me that I was covered for falling off the roof but not for hitting the ground.

Tommy Cooper

His psychiatrist is so expensive, all he gets for £25 is a get-well card.

Anon

There is no police like Holmes.

James Joyce

Does the name Pavlov ring a bell?

Anon

The quickest way to make a red light turn green is to try to find something in the glove compartment.

Gary Doney

I'm writing an unauthorized autobiography.

Steven Wright

I love flying – I've been to almost as many places as my luggage.

Bob Hope

Any man who grows to be more than five feet seven inches is a weed.

Frank Lloyd Wright

I have always wanted to write a book that ended with the word "mayonnaise".

Richard Brautigan

Why is the alphabet in that order – is it because of that song?

Steven Wright

The key to tennis is to win the last point.

Jim Courier

I would rather read a novel about civil servants written by a rabbit.

Craig Brown (of *Watership Down*)

George Burns is old enough to be his father.

Red Buttons

I installed a skylight in my apartment and the people who live above me are furious!

Steven Wright

Researchers have already cast much darkness on this subject and if they continue their investigations we shall soon know nothing at all about it.

Mark Twain

Cross-country skiing is great if you live in a small country.

Anon

My theory of evolution is that Darwin was adopted.

Steven Wright

After twelve years of therapy my psychiatrist said something that brought tears to my eyes – he said, "No hablo ingles."

Ronnie Shakes

There's a fine line between fishing and standing on the riverside looking like an idiot.

Anon

There aren't enough days in the weekend.

Anon

A lot of people never use their initiative because nobody ever tells them to.

Mary Allen

If in the last few years you haven't discarded a major opinion or acquired a new one, check your pulse – you may be dead.

Anon

Smoking will cure weight problems . . . eventually.

Anon

I took a course in speed waiting – now I can wait an hour in only ten minutes.

Steven Wright

Have you heard the one about the nudist who plays strip poker – every time he loses, he has to put something on.

Anon

I don't think God comes well out of it.

Virginia Woolf (on the Book of Job)

Is "tired old cliché" one?

Steven Wright

Backward ran sentences until reeled the mind.

Wolcott Gibbs

Just when you think tomorrow will never come, it's yesterday.

Anon

Aside from its purchasing power, money is useless as far as I'm concerned.

Alfred Hitchcock

People say that life is the thing, but I prefer reading.

Logan Pearsall Smith

Droughts are because God didn't pay his water bill.

Steven Wright

Never get into a narrow double bed with a wide single man.

Quentin Crisp

Give me a smart idiot before a stupid genius any day.

Samuel Goldwyn

What's wrong with being a boring kind of guy?

George Bush

I love California – I practically grew up in Phoenix.

Dan Quayle

Although he is a very poor fielder, he is a very poor hitter.

Ring Lardner

When it comes to ruining a painting, he's an artist.

Samuel Goldwyn

I would have given my right arm to have been a pianist.

Bobby Robson

If we don't succeed, we run the risk of failure.

Dan Quayle

I have my faults but being wrong isn't one of them.

Jimmy Hoffa

One word sums up the responsibility of any Vice-President, and that word is "to be prepared."

Dan Quayle

A lot of people my age are dead at the present time.

Casey Stengel

It's more than magnificent, it's mediocre.

Samuel Goldwyn

A lot of horses get distracted – it's just human nature.

Nick Zito

Anything that man says you've got to take with a dose of salts.

Samuel Goldwyn

He'll regret it to his dying day, if ever he lives that long.

Frank Nugent

Jim Morrison is dead now and that's a high price to pay for immortality.

Gloria Estefan

I got up more nostrils than there are noses.

Andrew Neill

Anyone who goes to see a psychiatrist ought to have his head examined.

Samuel Goldwyn

I'm for a stronger death penalty.

George Bush

I read part of it all the way through.

Samuel Goldwyn

There's always a choice of whether one does it last week, this week or next week.

John Major

The new West Stand casts a giant shadow over the entire pitch even on a sunny day.

Chris Jones

We are going to have the best educated American people in the world.

Dan Quayle

I'll give it to you in two words: im possible.

Samuel Goldwyn

I want to make sure that everyone who has a job wants a job.

George Bush

We are not ready for any unforeseen event that may or may not occur.

Dan Quayle

For this part of a lady – somebody that's couth.

Samuel Goldwyn

We shall have no coal industry if the miners are driven into the ground.

Claire Brooks

The United States has much to offer the Third World War.

Ronald Reagan (the mistake was repeated nine times in one speech)

Cauliflower is nothing but cabbage with a college education.

Mark Twain

A friend is someone who will help you move; a good friend is someone who will help you move a body.

Alexei Sayle

An Irish farmer, to cover the possibility of unexpected visitors, can often be found eating his dinner out of a drawer.

Niall Toibin

Noël Coward's wartime letter to Lawrence of Arabia (Aircraftsman T.E. Shaw, No. 338171):
Dear 338171, May I call you 338?

Free yourselves from the slavery of tea and coffee and other slopkettle.

William Cobbett

I called my landlord and told him that my apartment had terrible accoustics and he told me he'd caught them all long before I moved in.

Anon

When the guy who made the first drawing board got it wrong, what did he go back to?

Steven Wright

Light pranks add zest to your services, but don't pull the customers' ears.

Rules for Hotel Chambermaids,
Japanese Tourist Board

A moose is an animal with horns on the front of his head and a hunting lodge wall on the back of it.

Groucho Marx

Bambi – see the movie! Eat the cast!

Henry Kelly

The trouble with this business is the dearth of bad pictures.

Samuel Goldwyn

Nothing needs so reforming as other people's habits.

Mark Twain

Poets have been mysteriously silent on the subject of cheese.

G.K. Chesterton

Think of the old lady who had her petrol tank removed from her car and had it replaced with one that held litres instead of gallons.

Kenneth Manning

He's running a high temperature and his chest looks like a bad Matisse.

Noël Coward (of a friend with chicken pox)

A cucumber should be well sliced, and dressed with pepper and vinegar, and then thrown out, as good for nothing.

Samuel Johnson

Once, during Prohibition, I was forced to live for days on nothing but food and water.

W.C. Fields

Go and sing to them when the guns are firing – that's your job!

Winston Churchill (to Noël Coward)

Alcoholic: a man you don't like who drinks as much as you do.

Dylan Thomas

Nobody would wear beige to rob a bank.

Mickey Rose

A man could not be in two places at the same time unless he were a bird.

Sir Boyle Roche

If love is the answer, could you rephrase the question.

Lily Tomlin

He that but looketh on a plate of ham and eggs to lust after it, hath already committed breakfast with it in his heart.

C.S. Lewis

Television is for appearing on, not looking at.

Noël Coward

Right now, I'm having amnesia and déjà vu at the same time. I think I've forgotten this before.

Steven Wright

Dwn wth vwls.

Ruth Ollins

Gossip: hearing something you like about someone you don't.

Earl Wilson

Every time I start to think the world is moving too fast, I go to the Post Office.

Anon

I'm giving you the chance to redeem your character,
something you have irretrievably lost.

Serjeant Arabin QC

The single, overwhelming two facts were . . .

Paddy Ashdown

The doctors X-rayed my head and found nothing.

Dizzy Dean

This is the worst disaster since I was elected.

Governor Pat Brown

I probably have a different sense of morality to most people.

Alan Clark

They pushed their nomination down my throat behind my back.

J. Ramsay MacDonald

When I want your opinion I'll give it to you.

Samuel Goldwyn

Make-or-break situations, such as we have seen here, can sometimes make as well as break.

Robin Oakley

I wear very simple shoes – it is not one of my weaknesses.

Imelda Marcos

I can't see who's in the lead but it's either Oxford or Cambridge.

John Snagge

Every Tom, Dick and Harry is called Arthur.

Samuel Goldwyn

The trouble with referees is that they just don't care which side wins.

Tom Canterbury

Did you get a good look at my face when I took your purse?

> Accused thief who undertook his
> own defence (and lost)

What's the plural of "ignited"?

> Gaby Roslin

A verbal contract isn't worth the paper it is written on.

> Samuel Goldwyn

Chapter 6

SHARP RETORTS

Mahatma Gandhi was asked what he thought of Western civilization:
I think it would be a very good idea.

Snappy one-liners from (mostly) the rich and famous which need a little explanation.

Churchill was sent two tickets to the opening of George Bernard Shaw's new play with the message:
Bring a friend – if you have one.
Churchill replied that he was otherwise engaged but would like to see the play's second performance:
If there is one.

Calvin Coolidge, not known for his verbosity, was approached by a woman at a public function:
Mr President, I have made a bet with my friends that I can make you say at least three words to me during dinner.
You lose, came the reply.

On hearing that a judge had slept through one of his plays, Richard Brinsley Sheridan commented:
Poor fellow, I suppose he fancied he was on the bench.

At a Hollywood party, the actress Tallulah Bankhead met by chance an ex-lover whom she hadn't seen for years. She turned to him and said:
What are you doing here? I thought I told you to wait in the car!

Asked if he and his wife, Vita Sackville-West, had ever collaborated on anything, Harold Nicolson replied:
Yes, we have two sons.

When asked whether it was always sunny in Jamaica, Noël Coward answered:
Never at night.

Arguing against the necessity for a nation to be multilingual, Ralph Melnyk stated:
English was good enough for Jesus Christ.

Whilst in Egypt, T.E. Lawrence (Lawrence of Arabia) reluctantly attended a party hosted by a rather faded socialite who was famous for trying to befriend celebrities. Using the unseasonable hot weather as an opening, she sailed up to Lawrence saying:

92 today Colonel Lawrence! Imagine it! 92 today!

Many happy returns, madam, Lawrence replied.

During a speech, the politician Robert Menzies was heckled by a lady in the audience who shouted: I wouldn't vote for you if you were the Archangel Gabriel!

Without hesitation, Menzies replied: If I were the Archangel Gabriel, madam, you would scarcely be in my constituency.

Harold Nicolson was telephoned by the *Sunday Express* who wanted to know what was his wish for that year. He replied:

Not to be telephoned by the *Sunday Express* when I am busy.

John Wilkes was told by a voter that he would rather vote for the devil than for Wilkes. The politician replied:

And if your friend is not standing?

When asked if he believed in God, Noël Coward answered:

We've never been intimate.

Thomas Beecham heard that Malcolm Sargent, whose nickname was "Flash Harry", was conducting concerts in Japan. He commented:

Ah – Flash in Japan!

Whilst Noël Coward was in Australia, a gushing fan rushed up to him and asked him to say something funny to her. He leaned and whispered loudly in her ear:

Kangaroo!

On his deathbed, Voltaire was urged by a priest to renounce the devil. He protested:

This is no time for making new enemies.

When asked in an interview how his autobiography was progressing, Noël Coward replied:

Absolutely limping.

Asked why he had made a commercial for American Express, Peter Ustinov answered:

To pay for my American Express.

As the playing of the orchestra began to improve, Thomas Beecham commented to violinist Jean Pougnet:

Don't look now, M. Pougnet, but I think we're being followed.

It was eight in the evening when George S. Kaufman was asked, in the form of an invitation, what he was doing for dinner that night.

Digesting it.

The jazz musician, Zoot Sims, was asked how he could play so well when he was loaded.

I practice when I'm loaded.

Arnold Toynbee, author of *A Study of History*, which took him thirty-five years to complete, was asked by a journalist what had impelled him to devote that amount of time to a single work.
Curiosity.

Groucho Marx was asked if Groucho was his real name. He replied:
No, I'm breaking it in for a friend.

Did you mail that check to the judge?
                    Roy M. Cohn (in public, to his assistant)

Noël Coward was with a group of friends when someone announced that a boorish and overbearing acquaintance had "blown his brains out", to which Coward retorted:
He must have been an incredibly good shot.

When a waiter spilled soup on her dress, Beatrice Lillie complained:
Never darken my Dior again.

Alan Clark was asked by Douglas Hogg, then a junior Whip, how he was "keeping the new boys in order". He responded:
By offering them your job.

During his speech, President William Howard Taft complained that there was so much noise in the audience he could hardly hear himself talk, to which someone at the back replied:

It's OK, you're not missing anything.

Noël Coward was asked what sort of a child he had been:

When paid lots of attention, extremely lovable; when not, a pig.

In explanation of his dire performance in his Civil Service examinations John Maynard Keynes said:

I evidently knew more about economics than my examiners.

George S. Kaufman, drama editor of the *New York Times*, was asked by an agent how they could get their leading actress's name into his newspaper.
He replied: Shoot her.

Rebecca West discovered in 1945 that her name, along with Noël Coward and other luminaries, had been on the Nazi blacklist. Discussing it with Coward she commented:
Just think who we'd have been seen dead with!

Frank Underhill was asked how he could vote Liberal:
I just hold my nose and mark the ballot.

When asked, while an undergraduate at Oxford, what he did for his college, Evelyn Waugh responded:
I drink for it.

When Senator Wyche Fowler was asked whether he had ever smoked marijuana, he replied:
Only when committing adultery.

Tallulah Bankhead was asked by a male journalist if she had ever been mistaken for a man. Her reply:
No, darling, have you?

Rejection slip for a poem entitled "Why Do I Live?"
Because you send your poem by mail.

Eugene Field

An actress, worried about ageing, confided to a friend that she dreaded the thought of forty-five. The "friend" asked: Why, what happened then?

Singer: You know, I insured my voice for fifty thousand dollars.
Conductor: Really, and what did you do with the money?

Performers' responses to hecklers:

Look, this is my job – I don't turn up at your work and spit on the burgers.

Let me guess – tonight's square dance was cancelled, right?

Dost thou jeer and flout me in the teeth?

William Shakespeare

Peace, ye fat guts.

William Shakespeare

Away, thou issue of a mangy dog!

William Shakespeare

And put-downs:

I enjoyed your book , who wrote it for you?
Darling, I'm so glad you liked it. Who read it to you?

How about coming back to my place?
Will two people fit under a rock?

Hey, gorgeous, how do you fancy a good time?
Sorry, I don't date outside my species.

How do you like your eggs in the morning?
Unfertilized.

Is your husband a bookworm?
No, just an ordinary one.

No woman ever made a fool of me.
Who did then?

All's well that ends well – and vice versa.

Anon

Always remember you're unique, just like everyone else.

I didn't say it was your fault. I said I was going to blame you.

It may be that your sole purpose in life is simply to serve as a warning to others.

You are depriving some poor village of its idiot.

And finally, some pick-up put-downs:

Haven't I seen you someplace before?
Yeah, that's why I don't go there anymore.

Is this seat empty?
Yes, and this one will be too if you sit down.

Your place or mine?
Both. You go to yours and I'll go to mine.

I know how to please a woman.
Then please leave me alone.

I would go to the end of the world for you.
Yes, but would you stay there?